COLOR ENERGY

MEDITATION

for

Mind/Body/Spirit

VIRGINIA ALLEN McINTIRE, Ph.D.

COLOR ENERGY
For Mind/Body/Spirit

Copyright # TX 1-997-048
    1986 Library of Congress

For information:

Virginia Allen McIntire, Ph.D.
Beverly Hills, CA 90211

ISBN NO. 0-9634894-0-2

CONTENTS

*DEDICATED with love
To the members of the Workshop
who made us aware that color
is energy for Mind/Body/Spirit*

*"The truth must dazzle gradually or
every man be blind."*
                    Emily Dickinson

ENTER

This book is about color energy through meditation. If that idea is new to you, know that you will get no results crashing through the pages in one sitting to say "I don't feel a thing." You will only be numb from trying to absorb too much too quickly.

One of the big rewards of color meditation is the growing process of increased awareness that occurs as you comfortably mull over what you learn as you gently practice it over an extended period of time. You watch yourself grow as you try different shades and test new symbols, learning as you go what you need to discover about yourself and what works best for you.

Your color meditations bring an upbeat expanded feeling of being more alive, more creative and sensitive to all that is around you. It is this very awareness which makes life both inviting and successful for you.

Psychologists tell us any habit can be changed in thirty days, perhaps even less time with faithful adherance to the established mental pattern. Stabilize your intentions, work with the process, allow the new you to blossom.

If you have a half-and-half life now, bring it together with mind/body/spirit. These three participants create the trinity for a whole and well balanced house to live in. You don't have to struggle in an unfinished lop-sided life-house.

With mind/body you have the two fundamental visible elements which you have worked to improve all your life. Now you add the top and invisible element of spirit. With spirit the triangle becomes complete for the creative, dramatic quintessence of the whole being. The perfect balance is mind/body/spirit.

It is not our intent to delve into the psychic or clair-voyant field but rather to develop a higher state of perception for a daily working program to bring deep contentment and refined understanding of what color meditation offers for increased health, abundance, joy. Now through inner awareness your perception of the energy moving through this universe, either sound waves or color waves, is enhanced and acted upon. Today's operative words are "chemistry, vibrations, energy." Most of us fail to understand where these elements originate or how to use them for our own good.

Socrates told his students to lure a reluctant conscious to reveal its own purpose and thus lead the creature to a condition of sufficiency. Sufficiency is nice but it does not produce happiness. We also want peace, love, contentment and some sparkle.

How to lure a reluctant conscious? Go within to rediscover dreams, perfect goals, learn how to bring them to fruition. This takes a lifetime, but that is what you are working on now. As you go along make your abundance a little greener, more loving with pink, healthier with a blue shield. Lessons learned along the way become adventures in retrospect.

No one will ever give you this delightful growing life but yourself. Life makes the music but we are the choreographers and play all the instruments. If you hear nothing, see nothing, want nothing, do nothing, life gives you nothing. You get what you command.

If music is the sound of the universe, as we know it is, then color is its soul and energy of spirit. Color force enhances and essentially expresses what man thinks of himself and wants the world to know about him. Color tells us in red when the world is aflame, when the individual is angry and violent. Color warms and nurtures us with the gentle shades of pink for love and caring. Yellow ribbons are tied around trees when prayers of deliverance are offered with faith for the return of those in bondage. Green is abundance and blue for health, with both having prodigious records of achievement.

You are invited now to learn what color means and practice it for happiness and growth.

LIGHT ENERGY

While mankind did not create this amazing world, he has been given an infinite number of toys to play with, learn about, puzzle through to solve—if he can—the meaning of it all. Because the sounds and visions, the music and color is always here, he takes it for granted much too often.

These magnificent gifts are not only numerous but they encourage our progress throughout life if we use them for good. The vast array of colors, tones, tints, hues, shades, offer the opportunity for great experimentation in even the limited spectrum that we can see with human eyes. The bramble of confusion over what shades are "in" or high on the fashion list does nothing for the inner knowing of who you are.

Light, the source of all color, is an ever available power with wonderful potential when you begin to make it work for you. In this magical universe that makes mind/body/spirit the trinity of the individual, harmony is a law of the cosmos you can BEGIN to understand and utilize.

We know that light, or the lack of it, controls our energy and much of our actions. If we live underground in a smokey half-light, we will withdraw from life and be less creative. The syndrome called winter depression has to do with the lack of light and sunshine when shortened days create dejection, depression.

Psychologists have learned that this dullness and retreat can be changed or eliminated by placing the client beside a light screen for a given period of time each day. The light may be white or softly tinted in color that encourages the person to be uplifted psychologically.

Studies have shown that individuals working night shifts or changing hours, frequently can be rescheduled to more harmonious sleep patterns with less injuries on the job, more production and more comfort. We all set or reset our circadian rhythm according to when we are awake and when we sleep.

As laymen we are not concerned with the host of light waves bouncing off the earth to burn us up or keep us healthy. We know the sun burns when we lie in the sun at the beach, use sun block rather than umbrella for protection. Then there is x-ray, gamma ray, ultra ray and others we do not see but they are nonetheless extremely potent.

Today the effects of light and color are in research in many laboratories that analyze dreams, auras, even occult experiences which were untouchables to hard scientists a few decades ago.

Many years ago a creative man was trying to invent a machine that would rebalance a mind and body that were out of sync. One could plug into his machine and in a few minutes be relieved of all stress but when asked how often one had to have this frequency treatment, he said he had no idea. His machine probably had something to do with the sound waves that constantly bombard the earth, however he never mentioned color because no one gave credence to the effect light might have on our mental and physical moods.

For a period of time I worked in a small office blazing with an oversized fluorescent on the ceiling. I felt the reason for my discomfort there was because it was a passageway betwen two executive offices.

One day the light went out and I put a lamp on my desk and another on the wall table behind me which held magazines and a bulletin board above for press releases. Three days later the tube was about to be replaced as I came into the office.

"Never, never," I said because I had discovered the glaring light was the cause of my discomfort.

Soon company personnel began dropping by my office to discuss conflicts or knots in their daily chores. I no longer had to go to them because the gentle atmosphere made them feel more confiding and that someone was there to listen.

Photographers know that if you put too much light on the subject to be photographed it will "wash out" and lose color. We need to find the balance of light in every area of our living that makes for comfort, good production of our time with the least build up of tension. The right light decreases stress.

A California architect once told me that he never designed a home during the "all must be glass" period without providing a quiet room he termed a cave.

"Everyone needs a place to go where he can think or hide when the exposure becomes too bright."

This may not be true where the sun is not a constant daily event but we all need space for quiet contemplation. Intense light for long periods depletes the energy and drains our feelings so that we become grumpy and irritable. After heavy light exposure one may feel lethargic and sleepy.

Every individual has a different flashpoint and we can check ourselves by trying different light exposures and see the response in our temperature and activity range. Work for a balance that gives the most comfort for the longest period of time.

Driving on a hot day we can see color waves of heat dancing before our eyes. This shows that light comes as rhythmically as the tides wash the sands of the ocean. A good use of this dramatic energy will work surprising results once we learn what is best for our personal mind/body/spirit.

We fail to give light and color, which is the scattering of light, full credit for its capacity to effect change in our lives even though light is an elemental energy for survival. Science measures the wave lengths received in nanometers, each one equal to one billionth of a meter or one millionth of a millimeter.

The color that we have ability to see is said to be at the range of 380 to 780 nm, about an octave compared to sound waves. This electromagnetic energy charges our planet at the speed of sound, 186,000 miles per second.

The human being is poor indeed when he is unaware of the beauty and value to himself of all the color at his fingertips. "In living color" is truer than you may have thought. It is a loss when one does not perceive and therefore use what he would very much enjoy.

So far as we can learn it was the fourth century before anyone became interested sufficiently to question how human beings saw color. Then a Greek philosopher named Empedocles decided that color particles were given off by objects to pass through the eyes. Plato later reversed the idea and said vision is created in the eyes and then moves to the object to color it.

About the same time Aristotle had a theory and came to the conclusion that color diminishes in ratio to the amount of light it receives. In a dark room all strawberries are black.

An Arab physician recognized, about the fourteenth century, what happened was that a reflection of light from an object struck the eyes. Not too many people gave it much heed.

Finally around 1668 Sir Isaac Newton decided that color sensation is produced in the brain. He had carefully studied light reflection with a prism and saw the rainbow of colors produced, which were recombined into a second prism as light.

EXAMPLE

While all of the above was not clear to me at the age of ten, a startling experience proved the power of light. My mother and I were alone one night during a Nebraska summer thunderstorm. Loud claps of brilliant lightning lit up the room as angry rolling thunder sounded too close for comfort. I went into my mother's big bedroom and she placed a small mattress on the floor away from the open window, saying I might sleep there.   .

Suddenly a fierce rumble began and the growl accelerated like a locomotive bearing down on us. Mother and I sat up as the thunder seemed to drop a bomb on the front porch. A basketball sized fiery orange streak burst through the window, rolled along the floor and out the door to the hall. We were very frightened and mother reminded me that we were also grateful not to have been in the pathway of that very visible but unreal force.

The intense energy of that rolling fireball was never forgotten although it lasted only part of a second.

LIGHT MEDITATION

Color is the dispersed reflection of light. Somewhat like the old woman in the shoe who had so many children. . . . There are thousands of different shades and tints but most of us can name only a handful. There are exquisitely beautiful colorations, other shades are bland and drab, some hues suggest repression and have negative connotations.

The idea that light is a gift of energy to be given and received came as a large surprise to the Meditation Workshop. With that discovery it seemed necessary to present light in a variety of different formats they would enjoy.

Members were asked to decide if they wished to project a candlelight of power or become a thousand watt flood light. Light was used over and over as a theme, always in different ways, until members spoke of the luminosity they now acknowledged and appreciated. This law of the universe offered interesting possibilities which we explored.

They examined their urban attitudes about light in

contrast with perhaps a farmer, whose crops and animals depended heavily on light for growth and food. Urbanites, they agreed, think of light as buttons to be pushed in the office or home.

The gift of light, like other birthrights, was ignored because it was always available. We began to speak of the light force as an energy that changes feelings, emotions, creates moods, affects health, shifts the outlook on what life is all about in both good and evil ways.

Once Albert Einstein, as a young man, had wondered about light and tried to imagine what it would be like if he rode a light rod at 186,000 miles per second to earth from some distant planet. This passage was read to them from J. Bronowski's *The Ascent of Man* (page 247).

The meaning of passages from the Bible was discussed in relation to their prophecies and promises. "Let there be light and there was light," "I am the light of the world," "Ye are the light of the world." Genesis I: 3–4, John 9:5, Matthew 5:14.

The human form comes through darkness to birth into a world filled with light. It is said when we depart the physical plane we move again into that dark tunnel to reach the end filled with cosmic light.

"The self is not a substance endowed with consciousness as an attribute. It is pure consciousness itself, eternally perfect, absolutely free and intrinsically luminous."

We all respond to light according to our need, our understanding and faith. Some individuals are trapped in darkness of poverty, disease, or evil because they do not know how to use this energy to grow and become "intrinsically luminous."

More on light meditations is given in *Meditation Workshop*, my dissertation for a Ph.D. with a major in holistic psychology.

Following are excerpts from meditations on this subject which were perhaps two years after members had explored many avenues of self-lumination.

EXCERPTS:

LENA: Light was shooting across the sky and then began to flash off and on. I turned to my daughter and know I need to send her light. Then I knew the light meant that I can set her an example and I haven't been doing that. I saw Big Ben so maybe time is running out. It was very significant tonight.

JAY: I concentrated on mental light and the myriad meanings it can take on . . . like the light of understanding. I got excited with the idea of being able to give that light, transmitting it to others and how to do this. It's very subtle; this ability to give light to others impressed me deeply.

MAC: I went out several places but my space was never dark. It was light and alive and I received the feeling that I had to help someone. I still feel this need to help someone. Then I got the color blue, the first time I've had a lot of blue. It was magnificent, very bright. I felt it very nice and maybe I needed a healing. I will ask again. My hand has hurt for two weeks. Now

I realize all the pain is gone.

GAR: I took it literally after hearing the speed of light. I decided to climb on a beam of light and visit the universe. First, the light went through a prism of colors that was incredibly beautiful, incredibly vivid.

Then I came to pure white and sailed off, full of light energy. It was contrasted with the darkness I feel in the world. I seemed to be going the 186,000 miles per second but time stood still and there was no feeling of movement. There was this sense of creation, as Einstein said, light once created can never be destroyed. It belongs to the universe and forms a constant pool of light. The way we measure time is fantasy because we measure it by light, which is always out there even if not visible from dusk to daybreak.

CLAIRE: We are all so relaxed after our meditation. I too was on a light beam and went out swiftly. The beam looked like millions of thin glass rods, very thin and extended and made a whistling sound as I moved. It was primarily white with irridescent colors. I could feel the rods slipping past under my bare feet . . . nicely.

Then I found myself in an Indian village, a pow-wow with small children was going on. Don't ask me why.

LEADER: You're wearing a heavy squash necklace, you remember. Perhaps it was made in an Indian village. In meditating on the light try to stay with the light and don't go off on story trails.

CLAIRE: Usually I can do that and riding the beams

with pale colors was beautiful and the harmonics was a zingy sound like a violin sawing but I knew it was the rods slipping under my feet.

DEE: I saw a radar screen in front of me with beautiful colors. There were bits of light moving about that reminded me of little birds. Then I heard a silly song and the words would not go away.

LEADER: And the words are?

DEE: "High hopes, and the ant's moving the rubber tree plant and he can't but he's got high hopes. . . ." (Laughter)

LEADER: The subconscious tries to remind us that life is to enjoy.

CREATIVE ENERGY

Should anyone tell you there is a pot of gold at the end of the rainbow, reply that there is no end to the rainbow since it is a circle of 360 degrees.

I was forty years old before I learned that a rainbow looks like a colored doughnut in the sky. On a rainy flight from Oslo to Copenhagen the sky was ominous and very dark. Suddenly we flew into sunlight and there was a full rainbow rolling along at eye level with our plane. Its fullness startled me for no one had ever told me a rainbow was a bouncing ball of color.

Years later in a Scottish pasture near the castle, tourists gathered to witness an ancient jousting match. A sudden downpour interrupted and we ran for the trees. When the late evening sun returned it projected three giant rainbows on the distant sky. The tourists sang out but the Scots declared a triple rainbow of such behemoth size was not unexpected after a sudden rush of rain.

We moved back to the damp field where men on horseback continued their ancient ritual but for this

American the cosmic display was far more dramatic than the spectacle on the ground. It was a delight to see the grandeur of our universe so impishly displayed.

These pages are designed to show you how to bring color more richly and productively into your life daily, to show you how color affects everything you do in a variety of ways, be it auras, dreams, chakras, as well as your reactions at home, play, work, or personal relations.

It takes an audience to hear music, an audience to enjoy the dance, an audience to appreciate fine paintings. You are the audience required to listen, appreciate, enjoy the mental, physical and spirit that you have come to this earth to work and play with.

You expand this human being when you appreciate all you have been given and create new power for every part of the resources still dormant and untouched, waiting for creative energy to move out. As you expand your creative capacity, through being in touch with inner-knowing, you find that great good things are unlimited for you.

Dr. Rollo May in *Freedom and Destiny* writes, "Listening is our most neglected sense." Then he writes, "Most of us are so preoccupied with the noise, uproar, the cacophony of the modern world that we have no energy for constructive living. We long to pause. . . ."

"Pause" is that learning to listen so that we can appreciate who we are and make refinements in the many choices we have for good or evil. Hopefully the pause will bring out the creativity which identifies the best path to take, sends new signals for health, transposes old ideas into fresh ones. Listening will bring mind/body/spirit to consult for the purpose of forming independent ideas and flourishing bright beginnings.

It is spirit which tells us if we listen that it wants a clean house where friendly thoughts and loving deeds and happy talents will be welcome. Spirit watches and waits patiently but not always with satisfaction at our performance.

The fortunate thing about creative energy is that it can be produced not only unrestricted and limitless, but without any pressure or radical changes in activities until one is quite ready to accept whatever comes to encourage us through that meaningful pause. Now we listen to what we already know in heart but have refused to bring to consciousness.

Sometimes even as small a thing as the meaning of a word can make a tremendous difference in a skewed viewpoint. Some words like freedom and liberty we think of as synonymous but others are linked that have no blood relationship at all.

One set is prosperity and happiness. While we tend to believe that happiness shadows prosperity, that is not true. It may in fact work in the opposite fashion. When one comes to wealth it may disrupt whatever went before that was considered happy or content.

The rich may not be happy nor the happy have full pockets. What is necessary to bring the two together? Mind/body/spirit must be in balance.

Harmony and balance are not synonymous but they make a great team. Balance requires mental, emotional steadiness, the ability to perfectly maintain the influences and challenges you meet. Harmony becomes the result of this effort and is totally without any effort.

It is the reward, in a sense, of balance.

Let us clarify two more words that seem very close but have a subtle difference you will recognize and can use in your life. You have a choice for both happiness and joy. Happiness is the normal every day variety of acceptance and appreciation and activity when the world itself appears alive and well. It is leisure time or work that you love and a family to laugh and play and think with. It is lack of pressure.

Joy is deeper, wider, higher, with a more rewarding inward emotion that is exciting, challenging you to reach the gold medal. Joy creates an overflow of the "energy of awe" while happiness is more contented and has longer duration. Joy is like instant freedom, but then you want to settle back into familiar space.

Rollo May calls joy "Living on the razor's edge, the unfolding of life, while happiness promises satisfaction with one's present state, a fulfillment of old longings."

Joy is the newest dream, higher levels of consciousness never before attained, where you say in surprise, "I did it!" There is a new reality which two writers have described differently with the same idea.

Pierre Teilhard de Chardin described reality not only as the universe around, behind and in front of us, but more significantly, without ourselves. Alfred North Whitehead in *Adventures of Ideas* stated it, ". . . the human psyche activity thus contained the origins of precious harmonies within the transient world."

We all have this potential to create new energy out of what may seem nothing at the moment. We reach inward to seek what is already with us. Meditation is creative time that will lead you to those new beginings.

The best way to take that meaningful pause is to listen to what you already know.

You do this for yourself. The clergy saying prayers enmasse does not alert your spirit for only you can set the energy in motion.

Meditation is neither pushing nor pulling, which one sometimes tries to do with prayer. Rather it is placing yourself on notice that a pause is in order, may in fact be desperately needed to solve a long-time problem. Now is the time to listen. Create that space where mind/body/spirit can come together for consultation.

After this participation you feel relaxed, have recaptured some ease if not fully balanced but you know more meditation will surely solve your problem. Now you know what action to take.

There is a vast difference between listening to the silence and sitting quietly to rehash dirty loads of garbage from past failures, disapproval of others or hurts recalled. This is wasted time and debilitating for the mind/body/spirit. The trinity suffers when you tear mind and heart into shreds of discontent.

Listening in meditation is letting the mind go free, turning it loose to enjoy the opportunity to find new outlets, fresh answers, happy surprises for both mind and body.

One meditator told the Workshop after a silent meditation in which each one was to go inside and discover whatever they met there or learn what needed to be cared for, "I found a lot going on inside I had never given any thought to before. I have a lot of wonderful machinery and I heard my heart beat. All this goes on without my ever appreciating it before because I never had any complaints. I'm going to be better acquainted."

It is only fair to tell you that everyone did not get a pleasing response. One woman often came out of meditation with tears in her eyes and wept as she told what she did not want to feel. After several weeks of deep personal meditating on who she was it was time to admit that her life situation was wrong.

But she had no intention of changing it. She would keep what she had in spite of the negativity that blocked her real desire. Learning that she was reflecting the two sides of her personality and abusing the loving human being to maintain the greedy side of her nature she left the Workshop.

Life is like baking a cake. We create it by gathering to us the ingredients we blend together to go into the oven. There the mixture causes change and finally is tested as well done or a failure. The cake is of our making, delicious, crumbling or inedible.

Years ago my husband and I attended a new church that was different in philosophy from our traditional upbringings of Baptist and Episcopalian. We enjoyed the upbeat sense of well-being we found in this house of worship. Sunday gave me time to relax and often I would drift off into my own constructed fantasies.

What should I do with the job where I seemed stuck after ten years? Outwardly it was satisfying but far too routine to satisfy my inner needs for more activity, more creativity. At that time I called it mind-wandering, since I had never heard of meditation, and after church I might say, "I had a wonderful idea," or "something came to me that I'd like to try."

I had no idea why my mind rummaged in hidden

crevices for perhaps an idea set up years before or a plan which even had to do with my reason for coming to earth at this time in this place. Why was I here? The balance of the week there was no time for this very gentle creative energy to tap my consciousness.

Years later I found the answer when I attended one hour of silent meditation and asked why people attended when there was no communication between the guests. (See group meditation.)

You will learn to love the quiet time you give yourself. Let your meditation include your private color and the associations will surprise you, bring achievements that lead you to new awareness. As you work with color energy you will be made aware how much more color there is in the world and what it signifies. If everything green in the world disappeared we would have no abundance. We would have no way to even stay alive since rocks and earth are not edible.

To the five senses you may only partially make use of now, add a sixth called awareness. Some like to think of it as intuition but whatever the name, it adds a new sense of alertness and increases our ability to both get and give the most life has to offer.

Today we misthink that aerobics will make us healthy and whole. We misthink that the clothes we wear will make us happy. We misthink that a diet is our big problem. We misthink that money is the real answer to turn life around. Each of these may be helpful but not one of the above is the total answer for each is a limited idea and such a specific goal creates only imbalance.

We have all heard others say, "I know myself very

well," or perhaps "Of course I know what is best for me." Looking at one's face in the mirror every morning is no proof that we are remotely in touch with the possibilities and probabilities of where life will take us.

Many successful and happy people dismiss their good with, "I was lucky." We realize there is more than that. Their hard work, study of problems they faced and solved, acceptance of the good things which came along, happened because they were in tune with themselves. It was not because life was easier on them than any one else and in many cases their path was more difficult.

Find out who you are by getting in touch with the deepest patterns you have carved into your life, the dreams left unfulfilled, the chance life offers that you find hard to accept.

As you probe and consider and take the pause to find out what life really means to you, new good will present itself to test your interest and acceptance. The special awareness of what this means to you becomes increasingly part of your consciousness.

The example given here has nothing to do with color but it is the result of developing that keen sense of intuition through meditation that sensitizes mind/body/ spirit.

EXAMPLE

As you work with this book you will learn how to send loving color to surround someone who needs protection or encouragement. In the same manner you can send a message with no means of communication. This is not unusual or strange but merely the trained ability to use awareness in a way that is as yet unexplainable.

During a heavy work period I needed to contact my assistant who had gone on vacation to his home in Indiana. I had no idea how to reach him by phone but I sat by the phone a few minutes for each of three days and concentrated on reaching Peter.

To myself I thought, "Peter, get in touch. Call me now."

I spent no more than five minutes directing the message. "I need to know when you will be home. Please get in touch."

The third day I got a card telling me Peter would be home on Friday. Still I wondered why he did not telephone. Only later I realized it was not his style to telephone long distance.

When he called he said immediately with a laugh, "I got your message. I was driving down the street and saw your house number in front of me. I knew you wanted me to get in touch."

"Your card took three days," I complained.

He laughed again. "I thought your house number meant you just wanted to know so I wrote the card."

There have been other times when I knew Peter had an answer I needed although we never discussed the subject of mental awareness.

COLOR MEDITATION

The principle of color meditation is the transfer of light reflected from each color energy into the mind where body and spirit absorb and eagerly respond to this force of nature.

The body generates its own energy but also responds to what moves through and around it just as a swimmer knows when he is in the water but as it washes over him it does not deter his passage. As we react to heat, the atmosphere, vibrations constantly surrounding us, so too we react consciously or subconsciously to color.

For most of us it is not easy to carry a particular shade or hue in mind or even a favorite color sometimes. Much of our world we move through without ever seeing it precisely. Still you can teach yourself to be aware of a thousand different tints and hues if you desire to open your awareness in appreciation for what you have in your own environment.

If you decide to embark on the journey of fine color awareness, be prepared for changes to take place in both what you see and what you do as they dance and sing for you the choreographer.

You can learn to see a desired shade with closed eyes and hold the image in mind through meditation. Let love flow through you as you concentrate on a sheet of pink paper, feel it in your body, enjoy the sensation that is most nurturing. Or use a blue sheet to begin your meditation know that you are engulfed in healing.

You may use a swatch of a lovely colored fabric or hold a small object of the chosen shade in your hands or place it on a nearby table where you study it totally for a few minutes.

Sensitive individuals can "feel" color through their finger tips. We learned to do this in Workshop and began to practice after hearing the blind often can call a color after running it past the fingers. Each color energy gives off a different signal.

The Soviets worked with blind Rosa Kuleshova and called it dermo-optical when she reported "seeing" color through her fingertips.

When you work with color energy for a while you come to realize that more than visual image is important. There is a response from several senses when you taste color, hear it sing out to you, smell its fragrance or softness, touch it in mind without being nearby. Learn to let color float from heel to the crown of your head checking the sensations you achieve.

If someone says, "That blouse is strawberries and cream," you know he has taste awareness because he heeds the vibrations. Color associates with all kinds of feelings and reactions, suggests needs and resolves loneliness. One woman told me she had to do her meditations with her pink and blue lamb's wool blanket because it gave a security feeling she enjoyed.

Try to image your chosen shade with each of the five senses. What does blue ice taste like, how does it sound in cracking, how cool does it feel to your overly warm body?

If you lose your color after closing your eyes, open them and begin to image each sense again. It can take several sessions to teach yourself what to do to hold the color energy you wish to work with but know that it will happen if you persist.

If you are working with green and cannot retain the energy you may move to a green pasture or a pleasant row of emerald trees in mind and thus ultimately are able to find the essence of the dynamic purpose you wish to put into effect.

During your meditation all bodily processes slow to a relaxed state, rest lightly in consciousness. It feels like the moment before you go to sleep when all those driving thoughts are let go and you feel most at peace.

It is said a fifteen minute meditation is equal to an hour's nap. If you feel spent after a day's work, meditate a few minutes before going out in the evening and you will be able to enjoy it more. Now you sit comfortably with back erect, feet flat on the floor and hands loose in your lap. Hold your color to experience complete relaxation and enjoy this personal quiet time. You anticipate this deeper inner-knowing as you listen for what you will receive, lovingly, encouragingly. Let all feelings, emotions, be ready for the energy flowing in and out, giving and receiving, knowing and creating.

This color awareness tunes you in to the abundance

and brilliance, the joy and wonder that is all about you now. The subjective world of beauty and creativity fill the consciousness, which is mediator between body and spirit. The mind pauses to bring your being into harmony.

In later chapters you will find each color identified according to its essential force and quintessent characteristics. You can then decide what you need or desire to work with for your life's growth and happiness. With long deep breaths you learn to feel the color waves washing over you and moving inside to intensify your senses.

In the event you think just cruising past the color qualities without doing any meditative work will bring results, be assured that no results will occur. It takes meditation time to bring that deep level of inner knowing. Then color smooths the way and makes you more certain of your goals.

As a meditator with color, new awareness develops great appreciation for the abundance and brilliance of the world. You realize this ebullient confidence you are acquiring speaks from all your five senses.

The word spirit is breath from the Latin *spiritus*. You breathe this miracle of life in new dimensions. As we use the term spirit in these pages it has nothing to do with dogma or creed or religious order. Every living being has a spirit within that the dictionary describes as a vital animating principle held to give life to physical organisms. That is the sense in which we use it here.

When you were born you became a spiritual being just as you received a physical body containing a brain.

Think of your spirit as the happy-to-be-me guide

which makes its presence known when called upon, always ready with an honest answer to every challenge. It is the invisible but pure essence of you. You may think of it as conscience. It is much more.

Once you open the channel to be in touch, response is ready and certain of what is best for you. It may not agree if you have a sneaky or unsavory idea to practice but it is very much aware of the best that you can be and always eager to assist, to mitigate your anger or relieve pressure when the scene is heavy.

Once we become aware that all answers are not on the surface and may take patience to verify and put into action we can breathe easier. Rest, which means to catch one's breath, is experienced in meditation. The slower breathing reduces the body functions to alpha state, which is where we are when we first fall asleep.

As we are defining the terms used here we need to clarify the difference between prayer and meditation, often confused by clergy as synonymous. Actually they are very individual.

Prayer is reaching out to a compassionate Divine Source, either aloud or in silence to ask for intercession, conciliation, arbitration. Seeking help is the most often used and the poorest choice for prayer.

Meditation means to go within to silently listen and hear what spirit has to impart. What we hear may encourage or warn or suggest in guidance. When we learn to trust this inner knowing, all is well and we are not swayed by outer appearances or pressures.

Prayer is talking to God. Meditation is listening to spirit. A vast difference but they have in common the idea that there is a universal law which is available for communication.

Failure of the spirit happens when we despair of survival, be it a job, a career, a personal relationship. We give up because we no longer care to try to rise above the challenge. If we have chosen a wrong path and refuse to admit it, spirit recedes and we find nowhere to turn. Spirit imparts the energy and activity to move forward and not as the Arabian proverb says, "Be careful not to move your feet off the carpet."

Rollo May writes, "The language of spirit increases as it is shared . . . the language of spirit is image, symbol, metaphor, myth and these comprise also the language of freedom."

Meditation opens wide the subjective world of beauty, creativity, happiness through spacious awareness and all this belongs to every day. Do not accept this participation for only weekends or birthdays or Christmas. Learn to enjoy it every day of the week.

What have you done when you became anxious or fearful? Take a valium? Another drink or drug? Over fifty million prescriptions for valium (with all the other mood-changing drugs) have been given to relieve depression or misery in one year's time.

Whatever it takes to return us to harmony and balance is not in a pill or drug. Our anxiety is trying to tell us that there is work to be done, an activity needs correction, a choice should be made. The answer comes after moving boulders from our path, climbing moutains to get to the other side where our safe comfort is found.

You may find after meditation that nothing seemed

to happen although you notice that you are more relaxed, less irritable, or encouraged about something you thought was lost. This is a nice beginning in opening the channel; let spirit be a participant in bringing your trinity together in balance.

As your meditations continue gradually other things move away because they are not part of your new good and replacements come with new friends, better health, more peace.

Most of us waste energy and time pawing over debris that should have been discharded years ago. We need that space to find a new outlook, try another tune and seek a fresh approach that becomes an adventure in living. When old fears are dislodged the good begins to flow, slowly at first, then in a fountain of rainbow colors.

We live in a universe exquisitely designed but we never try to circumvent the laws by which it operates. We never can in the end.

During our Workshop in the UCLA campus a young lawyer came to fill a lonesome evening. Three years later he came to my home one day to tell me that gradually he discovered in meditation that he had love to give and there was no reason to be lonely. He was now happily married because he learned something about himself.

We know there are many different forms and ways to meditate but two Western forms are very different and should be mentioned for your considerations because as you go along you will hear more and more ideas about what is best for you to practice. Only you can decide what makes you the most comfortable and brings results.

Both the approaches given below are for healing physical problems and one is negative while the other is positive. However, followers of both forms declare their system works wonders and we have to know we are all different and so this is probably true.

By the first, the patient meditates on the idea that he will go within his body and tear out and destroy diseased cells, then bombard the damaged area with wellness. This is a psychological approach to replacing bad with new good.

A more affirmative technique for self healing in meditation is to take all the energy away from the disease. We do not let it control our thoughts or actions because we know there is a cure for all illness when the mind is healed.

This is what Norman Cousins did when his doctors told him that he was terminal. He turned away from the disease and healed himself in quiet time with knowing there was an answer. His story is told in his book *Anatomy of an Illness.*

Work with your doctor, then work with yourself to flood the mind with reassurance that your light shines in wellness, image wholeness, in all three essences that make you a special individual, mind/body/spirit. It is because something is dangerously out of harmony that you become unable to cope with normal activity and take to bed.

The metaphysician knows that miracles happen because they are only laws that science has not yet found the answer for. Some day they will learn to accept laws that cannot be replicated in the laboratory, as love cannot be proven or disproven.

Suppose your need is for physical healing and you read that the healing color is blue. You feel blocked because you have never cared for the color blue. You have nothing against the sky or the ocean but the color is just not for you.

The world certainly needs a lot of healing and could it be that is why we have so much of this blessed color around us? Examine different shades and tints of blue, knowing there are thousands of shades of this one primary color. Or consider what happens when you add a smidgen of green and create a gorgeous turquoise that you do find bright and cheerful. Or add a drop of red to blue and mix with white for a gentle lavender that is warm and loving. Keep blue as the basic color and adopt your new shade for a harmonious and healthy meditation pattern.

Awareness of color is never rigid and uncompromising but rather very flexible. It opens new doors of multiple choices for your enjoyment and success for your special quiet time.

When you walk along a tree-lined hill you now see many shades of green from emerald to citron, each abundantly exhibiting the freedom you and each living thing has to expand, to grow, to be the best of whatever we choose. A friend said she never noticed her tree-lined street until someone told her that the waving leaves were clapping for her as she passed by. Now she smiles and nods a greeting in return as she heads for work.

After you have read the chapters on what each color energy signifies, begin a color notebook to record your meditations and how each of the five senses reacts to your chosen shade that is working in your behalf. Start with the easiest color and a simple desire so you can test for yourself the result. If you try to solve the world's problems when you've done no work on them ever before, it will be too much. Begin with the idea that each small dream realized makes the big one get in line for later. Each success encourages the next step.

When you bring color and meditation together the growing awareness surprises you. Contemplation and sensation join forces in a fresh way for this technique designed for wholeness and harmony in your life.

In your notebook record the time of day you mediate, the way you feel before you begin and what results are received. If it is merely a quiet time and nothing much happens at first, don't give up. You cannot graduate before kindergarten. Continue to study color and shades you like and what they signify. Gather your swatches of fabric or sheets of clear and lovely paper. The standard 8½ by 11″ sheet can be purchased in packages of many colors where children's papers and colored pencils are sold. In other words, build up seeing more color around you and your awareness will expand.

When you pick a meditation shade, stay with it long enough to feel submerged in the energy it offers and you begin to see it as you move through the day in unexpected places. Know every time you see it that it is telling you inside, "Enjoy, be encouraged, you can do it!"

Sometimes a shy or insecure person will say, "I'm going to send my daughter love. That's the place for me to begin." Later she may come back to tell us that her daughter telephoned and it was the first time in months. This sense of accomplishment and knowing she had the ability to make it work is a happy experience that helps one move on to the next step.

In considering the value of color energy author S.G.J. Ousley lists seven intrinsic elements that relate to the human spirit. They are:

1. A physical or material element

2. Vitality giving power

3. Psychological element

4. Harmonious element that unifies

5. Specific healing element

6. Element of inspiration and intuition (creativity)

7. Spiritual higher consciousness element

We see that he recognizes color as a strong binding force for mind/body/spirit. Life is improved, made harmonious and inspired with new vitality and creativity we all want to find and put to good use.

WHAT CAN COLOR DO?

Color is:

1. alive and engaging
2. demonstrative and emphatic
3. revealing and responsive
4. vigorous and powerful and energetic
5. timid and shy and retiring
6. repressive and lost and cold
7. aware and unconscious
8. strength and debilitating
9. appealing and nurturing
10. inviting and repelling
11. reflective, sensitive and moody
12. waves and rhythms and pulsating
13. dominating and aggressive
14. polished and pretentious
15. tender and graceful
16. mystical and intuitive
17. uplifting and happy

If color is all the above, each in its own time and place, don't you think the understanding of the right use of color can help you to reach a higher state of consciousness by working with the color principles?

FROM WHITE TO BLACK

White light has been called the cosmic day, too powerful for us to see with the naked eye. Its brilliance is unreal to earthlings but depicted in the movies as surrealistic space. Every child today believes this brilliance of the unknown is out there somewhere and one day they may see it.

White is not technically a color but opaque light that reflects off of it all the colors available to the human eye. This glint of color comes alive when it is reflected off a prism or crystal. One of the reasons we prize cut crystal is because it dances with sparkling color according to its surroundings.

Do we realize that the human being also responds and becomes alert or dulled according to the colors in his own surroundings?

In Western civilization opaque white signifies purity and the innocence of the bridal dress but that is rapidly changing. The idea of white representing cleanliness in hospitals, schools or institutions has also shifted to softer healing shades that are more pleasing and compassionate. In its pristine virtue and idealism white is said to drain energy.

Eastern philosophy prefers white for burial as one makes a transition to a new life. Many reporting life after death scenes recall a long dark tunnel which led to a brilliant cosmic light at the far end. As they moved toward the light they were either told to go back or experienced a sense of someone needing them and they asked to be returned to life.

Those individuals who have had the life after death experience insist that their life has been changed in some profound manner and they feel relieved of old superstitions and cleansed of fear about death. Now they have a spiritual sense that they understand life is eternal.

Since you and I are not totally spiritual beings yet, we need to engage in color for the enhancement of our lives. We can make it brighter, make it more fulfilled and joyous than before when we understand the tools are here if we use the technique. Make this an exhilarating passage from birth to death because you have the gifts of five senses to enjoy color.

BLACK

This rejector of light is negative because it blocks the color waves and therefore the energy we may use and enjoy. The dungeons of the mind are without light, therefore unenlightened. Black is a dense mass that bars new thinking, new improvement and robs other colors of their energy when blended to subdue or negated their vitality and bright promise. A small dot of black on the artist's brush diminishes the color purity forever.

Moody black in the pitch dark on a lonely road produces not only mystery but even terror in the mind if we lose our innate sense of security and protection. Black stands for authority and restriction when it is worn.

We know that soft and reduced lighting in a room adds a relaxed sense of mystery and creates fantasies. In a room darkened for hours with a television, may give a sense of depression before one goes to bed. Do something to change this mood level before you retire.

Many restaurants are very dark inside for two reasons. One has to do with cleanliness, which is not our subject here but has been recognized by those who go into restaurants to photograph with very high powered lights. The second reason eating houses are low lit is to make one less aware of other diners, creating a more intimate atmosphere with table companions.

Never use black for a meditation because it has no response for one seeking health, friends, success, or a brigher outlook. If the umbrageous presence of heavily muddied colors,you feel sucked into the dregs of negativity. In the aura such spaces denigrate the health and/ or personality of the individual. More in the chapter on auras.

In the chapter on dreams you learn that dreams which frighten or turn into nightmares are often during nightime scenes of being lost or being attacked by something not identified in darkness.

GREY

Grey is a shadow shade, a color in retreat if it includes only black and white. An offspring of black, like its darker source, smokey vague shades lack vitality. Flat and lacking courage, grey refuses to articulate what it stands for if anything. It is a docile mongrel among the family of color.

Grey green, as with grey blue, diminishes the healing and abundance which is available energy we want to use. A smokey shade of rose, sometimes called ashes of roses, is demure, less sure of its promise of love and devotion. Every color loses energy and intensity when greyed. It may become a dirty, lackluster neutral whether it appears in the home or on the person.

Working in grey areas for long periods of time can make one feel low in energy and less alert. No one needs live in a grey world and the run from black to white and all the steps between are not good for meditation.

Stay with your chosen color even if you must keep your eyes open for meditation and this will help you. As you become more sure of yourself in your intention to improve or change, you will then be able to close your eyes and see the energy flow. This is particularly important if you have many dark thoughts about a situation that needs to be rectified and resolved in harmony.

If you find yourself moving into darkness during meditation, open your eyes to absorb the color you are working with. Hold that positive energy message to impress the subconscious with your true intentions

Turn the thoughts around until the inner vision sees the good and affirms that what you seek is natural for mind and heart. Then it will be easy to visualize your color whenever the wrong impression rises to mind. Listen for the color that communicates your good to you.

SILVER

Light grey turned to silver has a redeeming quality because it is illuminated with scattered light that brings it alive. There is a radiance and glow with polished silver or even when it is dulled or hammered. The silver glow remains.

Silver is much desired by many because it suggests wealth and is used to coin money in many countries. However silver is an accent in the home where it brings special luster with a tea set, a picture frame, or silver flatware set on a pretty table.

Now we put black and white aside and begin our work with each color and its meaning for us in terms of energy, dynamic power and to strengthen our desire to make life the very best.

RED HEAT WAVES

Because you know that red rays are the most ener- gized on the color chart you realize that red is a warn- ing light, the quickest color to grab your attention. It is also the theme color for war and hostility, blood and violence.

The most sinister evils deal largely with black and red as negative symbols of passion and disaster. Con- sciously or subconsciously we react to this blatant tone. It is as different from the other colors on the chart in implication as a loud gong is to a string of chimes.

It requires your attention whether you read the meaning there or not. Now we understand why many restaurants are awash in red right down to the glasses and napkins on the tables, if not the tablecloths them- selves. When you enter your level of excitement rises and you feel suddenly hungry. In coffee shops the hot color tends to keep the customers moving faster.

The fiery color is the one that makes the angry indi- vidual say, "I'm burned up at what was said." There is a sense of being out of balance when one is over- charged with such negative feelings and a continuation of the pain will lead to physical illness that one does not need.

A red insignia on a military uniform or a red jacketed parking valet will impress you, consciously or otherwise, with an assertive intent. While red makes a lovely and striking evening dress or a daytime suit, it is not a color we can handle for all-time wear.

The red heart of Valentine's Day is the symbol of life's energy. In large amounts it is best reduced to a gentler show of devotion in joyous pink as the heavy saturation of red is reduced from its authoritarian implications.

The photographer has learned that red is a very dense color on film and takes more light to bring it into harmony with blue and green, which give off less energy, in a photograph that includes many shades. When light strikes black it easily greys off while red clings to its saturated base, requiring more light to reduce it to a rosey hue.

The waves of light are like the waves of sound, rising and falling as the universe whirls on axis. In a smaller way our consciousness tries to harmonize colorations, making what the eye sees and the ear hears into musical notes rather than crashing cymbals and shattering shrieks.

The corporeal body is dense and much that we see is not truly perceived, while the subtler subconscious takes in a message that may be color confused or uncertain about our intentions.

We need go no further before suggesting that red is not for meditation because of its contentious aggressiveness.

Once in calling on a homemaker she told me that she was growing concerned over a newly decorated bedroom. Her husband's favorite color was red so she put the room into red. Now many arguments were tearing them apart and seemed to begin in the newly decorated bedroom.

The red energy struck me like a hot fire as she opened the door. This bedroom was indeed total heavy red from carpet, walls, bedspread, lamp shades with no relief in sight except a dark dresser. When the wife was convinced that she should cut back her color and break up all the hot energy into only accent points, the temperature was reduced to a pleasant relationship once again.

Think of red as a firestorm that is always on the move. If someone gives you a red billfold, you can be sure your money wil have a difficult time staying in that billfold. I tried it once when a beautiful gift of a red billfold came to me. I found that money seemed to just disappear and finally realized what was going on. I returned to my leather billfold to match the handbag and the problem was solved. You may say you are not that color sensitive but if you snoop around at what is going on in your life with color you'll have some surprises.

EXAMPLE

In the late 1960s a stranger asked if I had ever heard a story like the one he was about to tell. Since I worked with color he thought it possible but improbable. I had not at that time.

The gentleman was flying across country and there developed a problem as they were about to land. The captain came on the intercom and told the passengers it would be a hard landing, to fasten seat belts and put their head down between their legs.

After the instant realization that he might die, this man had no time to be afraid because as he closed his eyes brilliant flashes of light seemed to surround him. The light was intense and unreal, like no colors he had ever seen before. He felt elated at the brilliance, surrounded by illumination which he tried but could not understand.

The next thing he knew the plane slid on a sea of foam laid down on the runway and he was aware of not even a small bump as the plane came to a stop.

"I've never been able to see those brilliant colors since then and I don't know what happened," he said.

At that time none of us at the table had heard the expression "out of body experience" or knew about auras that might expand or diminish at the approach of danger. Today so much more needs to be learned about these spectacular phenomena.

WARM SHADES

PINK

One of the most gracious, gratifying and generous colors for your meditations is filled with winning energy.

Pink is the energy of love, that happy combination of strength and passion drawn down with much white for purity and tenderness. Pink denotes all the positives we associate with love when we give compassion, thoughtfulness, loyalty on the total range from adoration to friendly endearment.

Whether they needed personal comforting and nurturing or wanted to express their love for another, Workshop members reached for love with soft rosy shades.

Pink is very effective for evening meditation to wash away the harshness of a bashing day. It releases tension and polishes the hurt away. We know the world is all right but most of our challenges are with other people. Only people tear us apart, for human beings have free will and when they are unhappy, often feel the need to make others pay for it.

With this happy, caring color we find a way to be forgiving and to forgive ourselves. Questions are no longer important, only that we have answers which soothe the pain and release the anguish before it becomes magnified.

Use pink energy as your personal love note for it can never be used up. The more you give the more you have. In your color notebook write out love messages to send that reflect your feelings for yourself and others. Before you meditate repeat those words several times and feel the glow inside that makes a beautiful meditation.

There will always be enough and to spare. If knowing this has been hard to accept, begin to work with the idea in meditation that you will both give and receive love, health, abundance and happiness. Don't be afraid to accept the abundant share that has been prepared for you.

Write in your notebook how you feel now about love and what possibilities you have to give it and enjoy it for yourself. Examples might be:

1. I know there are no problems too large for the universe to solve. I want to resolve this small personal dilemma in the best possible manner. In order to accomplish this I send love with genuine consideration to _____ . I surround him/her with a pink cloud of love and forgiveness. I see what has come between us has melted away and replaced with understanding which is loving and thoughtful of each other.

2. Because I know how to give love I also must receive it and not be fearful of accepting what is rightfully mine to have and enjoy. Love comes to me with

tenderness, kindness and I am in the midst of the energy now which is everywhere present.

3. I send love where it is needed and know it is received because the pink energy moves softly through the universe and is never lost. Surround my dear ones with love and safety.

ORANGE

A healthy glow of warmth is orange with its bright aggressive energy that combines the activity of red with the more thoughtful spirituality of yellow.

With two such progenitors a clear orange energy is both strong and pleasant, supportive in arousing a sluggish situation or polluted attitude to get intentions recognized and acted upon.

This active color is best in small portions with clear orange tones required for happy results. Too often orange is muddied and diluted with dark shades that turn it mustard or brownish and make of it an outcast with negative implications. The mood of orange is clearly bright and sunny for it is an outspoken member of the warm side of the color chart.

Cold hands should try holding something warm for a few minutes and feel the heat coming into fingers and mind. If you have a problem with cold fingers and toes, ask someone to knit you mittens or socks in bright orange. You can feel the temperature as you put them on and this will help you understand how color energy works for you.

CORAL

Reducing orange's heated energy with white makes it a more acceptable range of shades to work with for those who want it in home decorating or as wearing apparel.

There are many shades of apricot, tangerine, mandarin orange, coral and the pale tints where only a hint of orange remains. As you add more white the energy of the base color reduces but in this case the fresh and lively feeling is never lost. All the shades which have a clear orange beginning are on the happy side of energy.

Also we have the copper and brass luster to include in this bouquet of buoyant family members.

There was much publicity in which diseased individuals who had little hope of finding a cure were told to wear copper bracelets. We do have copper in our bodies and need it in very small amounts and there are presently studies being done to determine the value of copper in the system. The most significance a copper bracelet can have is that it reminds you to believe you can be healthy and the reminder encourages you to think wholeness.

A person with a consistently negative temperament seldom chooses any shade of the corals to be around him in home or wardrobe. The natural friendliness and buoyancy of the shades suggest love and creativity and openness not acceptable to the restricted personality. Since there are stronger healing energies available to you, leave these shades for light-hearted fun times.

YELLOW AND GOLD

Do you wear gold jewelry because of its show-off qualities or because it is the color of intellect and spiritual attributes?

Since yellow is the color of intellectual awareness, it holds a very high place in our minds. We used yellow ribbons when we had no other way of expressing our desire to bring hostages home and we sought higher wisdom to resolve our challenges.

We know that the saintly figures of many religions are depicted with the golden halo around the head to show wisdom as leaders of a breakthrough in some new moral teaching.

When one chooses yellow for meditation it indicates a reaching for knowledge, a desire for creative wisdom and good judgment in making decisions. It may mean a spiritual mission of mind or body that one feels called to fulfill in service to mankind.

We know also that gold has been the reason for many negative events throughout the world as long as human beings had the mind for avarice, greed, jealousy, or coveted something of that color.

Years ago I went to a small church in Spain which had been desecrated by the peasants uprising several years before. My guide pointed out that when the oppressed revolted they always went first to the church where they smashed ritualistic elements and then stole the golden altar pieces. This gold represented the repressive leaders of their community and church. Thus the subconscious mind reacted to allow the peasants to destroy their own community.

Yellow has been called divine clarity. Keep your yellow clear and gold unblemished if you meditate with these prize tones. Intangible qualities can be expressed through all colors but it is special with yellow for enlightenment, illumination, wisdom, discernment of the unknown.

If one works with muddied or scarred shades there will be no positive meditation for the energy is gone or severely blocked. This understanding came as members found that they need clarity of tone first in order to establish true communication with the inner spirit.

THE HEALING COLOR

BLUE

While we know that all color is coded energy that pulsates through our brain, we do not know why we respond to color as we do either positively or negatively. Neither do we know all there is to learn about how we respond to sound although much more has been done in that field.

Color is beginning to be recognized as a valued component in the lives we lead although we react differently according to our background, environment, culture and sensitivity.

I've not read nor heard of any scientific reason why blue in meditation will bring us back to center when we are stressed and off balance. In *The Physics of Chemistry and Color* author Kurt Nassau lists examples and gives the causes of color in technical terms not for these pages. Still it is not too technical to ask the question about why our planet is blue since our astronauts described it as "a small blue ball hanging in space."

Why is seven-eighths of the planet covered with waters of ocean, river and stream and why is it blue?

Why is the sky for 360 degrees from horizon to horizon also blue? Have you ever wondered who chose this coloration to surround us? Why not yellow or brown or buff? Why is blue so easy to live with?

A simplified version from Nassau's book is that "After part of a beam of light has been absorbed in a solid, some of the energy lost from the light may be found in increased atomic and molecular vibrations and rotations. . . . This type of selective absorption . . . is responsible . . . for the very pale blue observed when pure water or ice is viewed in large bulk . . . a variant of light scattering."

Have you ever asked: Of all the colors in the rainbow why is water blue? You may never have heard that colors have special energies and working with this healing blue is too often an ignored blessing.

Because blue is the calm, tranquil primary, it has been described as reserved, aloof, restrained, even cold. That is far from the truth when you begin to examine the varied possibilities it has for doing good in our magnificent world. While blue maintains its serenity this respected color uses its prestigious presence and the strength of its vitality to heal, cleanse, restore.

Blue water makes what is soiled clean, blue makes what is polluted fresh, while watering the crops that they may become abundant to feed us all. Think about a world so constructed that it heals itself when allowed to do that.

The color rays which flow constantly around us are programmed to help us resolve the destructive emotional trauma we set ticking and to silently repair and renew the stress in divine order. Many people have told me stress is required but the answer to that is: Watch a tree grow, look at the flowers in the garden, see a pony racing after its mother in the paddock. All can do well with no stress for growing is exciting and exhilarating, not painful, if we stay in harmony with our universe.

We travel to the mountains to be closer to clear blue skies and then to the beach or take a cruise to feel refreshed by the blue waters. All this in the name of relaxation, rest, renewal. There are at the present time several groups which charge fancy prices to allow you to come to the wilderness areas or high mountains just to be alone with yourself and find peace.

Peace and harmony are not that elusive when you know how to sit in one place and meditate in a pattern that accomplishes all that you wish to bring to your life experience.

"Getting away from the world" with others trying to do the same thing is not expensive if you know how to sit in your favorite chair and reach for that inner-knowing which is suppressed but will float free when released with meditation.

The urbanite is not as fortunate as the farmer or sailor or ranger if he has not learned to enjoy the sky on his way to work and let the blue healing energy surround him like a soft cloud. I missed the double decker buses when they left Wilshire Boulevard in Los Angeles though at the time had no reason for being sad. It was not to see the street scenes which were the same basic sights for some sixty thousand rides. It was the sky that I missed most.

If you work at home or are confined, meditate recalling a favorite lake or playground in the woods where it seemed joyous to be alive. Go back to a precious scene and draw the blue energy of peace that will bring health and happiness today.

All light is filled with blue rays which are particularly noticeable as a blue reflection or shadow is cast during the cooler months of the year. In summer heat it is the dusk that brings relief from the warmer rays as soft blue shadows emerge to add their mystical sensitivity.

In my old Roget's Thesaurus color is listed as one of the organic matters, together with life and death. Have you ever considered color as organic, that stuff of which life is made? A doctor in the last century experimented with color for healing and called blue the oxygen of life . . . something we dare not live without. Now think of this cool side of the chart with one color we can indeed not do without.

This blessed primary color has a wider range of hues and tints and blends than any other basic color. There are literally thousands of blues plus the range from a touch of red or pink added to give a blue-lavender or a dash of green for the family of turquoise.

For meditation we chose a personal shade somewhere in mid-range of clarity and saturation for our healing. Choose your personal shade with the knowledge that you may want to lighten or darken your blue healing light as you grow and change in consciousness. The deep cobalts and bright electric shades are a bit heavy for a beginning but then the baby blue and blue-lavender are too soft with little energy so stick to the clear middle palette.

Find the shade most pleasant to yourself to restore,

refresh, renew and if you find it too strong in intensity, add white to soften the flow so that it moves gently through your daily activity and is reinforced in meditation.

If you have ever spoken of "feeling blue," turn that around to recognize blue energy as affirmative because "blue feels wonderful as it brings wholeness and balance into my life."

Noble blue is healing for the mind/body/spirit which is all of you. Should we learn to recognize balance in our lives as the most needed quality to discount stress and fatigue, we then would be engulfed in healing blue.

Try to fix your shade in mind so that when you close your eyes it is there. Let your color be the liaison to turn sorry-for-myself into glad-to-be-alive. Use the healing sky as you go to work or see another in a blue dress which reminds you that you are a whole and happy individual. Each time you encounter any shade of blue reinforce your knowing that these rays are for your use and enjoyment.

Becoming color sensitive will add much to your intuitive awareness as your world becomes more colorful and alive. When you have chosen a particular color or shade for meditation your thoughts begin to move with fresh awareness in that direction. For some the shade moves us into a matching colored scene or event, for others it remains with the shade to absorb the pleasant infusion being received. Whatever happens, let that take over and flow it into harmony for the vibration is for your good.

Begin your healing meditations with the agreement

to yourself that you will accept wholeness as you align with universal energy through this healing color.

First there may only be a sensation of deep relaxation, the feeling you have had a restful nap. When this happens you know you are relieving stress and asking the body to believe in good health. As you move along the evidence will become more reassuring that you are on the way with your healing color.

Everyone makes the choice whether to use nature's restorative powers or go with chemicals and drugs. The prescription route is the reason many medical men say, "There is no cure, only remission for today's diseases."

Color therapist Edwin D. Babbitt (1824–1905) called his years of experimentation with healing "chromotherapy." Those who did not accept his beliefs he labeled "crystalized conservatives." It is necessary to mention that those who cannot accept any natural healing are refusing because illness brings amenities and attention that would not otherwise be given. What a frightful price to pay for attention, especially when color energy has the audacity to challenge decayed obsessions, a damaged and abused body that should be free of pain.

The deeper truths of color's potential are only brushed by when someone says, "I feel very relaxed when I come into the blue room," or "I wore a red suit today because I needed a pick me up."

Earlier healers giving coloration treatments have published examples of the rays they chose for specific diseases, however there is no verification that any one set worked better than another and they disagree with what we learned and report here.

We all see and feel differently about color and you must find what is best for yourself and work accordingly. This is to serve as guidance we hope will be of genuine benefit.

In Workshop we began with no specific program as we tried to adapt this delightful energy for inner knowing and self awareness to resolve the challenges presented over several years. We first recognized the value of color and the positive and negative possibilities that each energy seemed to offer. Then we accepted and enjoyed the bountiful, beautiful world we found around us and appreciated the opportunity to participate.

Do not expect any color or any meditation to do for you what you are not willing to do for yourself. If your eating habits are atrocious, your body abused wtih weight, lack of exercise or overwork, correct the obvious needs with determination and enthusiasm because you have a new program that will add to your happiness.

When you select a shade to work with, stay with it for the weeks necessary as it responds gently to test your sincerity. The flow of energy appears to increase as the subconscious accepts your endeavor to change and improve.

The best health plan you can have is to take the time each day for the long pause of inner knowing, renewing faith in your own wholeness and placing yourself in harmony with your surroundings. Attune yourself to divine protection and affirm the energy which flows through mind/body/spirit every day.

Katherine Kuhlman the evangelistic healer said, "The healing of the spiritual body is the most important of all . . . even though the body (physical) may be irreparably impaired for the spirit can make it whole."

One evening at Workshop members were asked to tiptoe inside themselves and listen to that physical body, hear what it said. One report said, "I was flying over blue water, the Pacific I think, and there was a lazy seagull coasting along nearby. He knew where he was headed and I got the message that I need to know better where I am going. I don't have to be in such a hurry all the time. I understand that now . . . a bird taught me."

Learn to use all your five senses in meditation. Rediscover sound, taste, touch, smell, sight, and then add feelings to the list. The emotional response will tell you quickly if what you experienced was pleasurable or asking for a change somewhere in your life and activity.

EXAMPLE

A magazine sent me to report on a man who had made a great success raising money for a children's hospital. As we sat down in his office for the interview he responded to my first question by saying, "I'd better tell you the story of how it happened."

He had been a young millionaire in Kansas City and lost everything he owned very suddenly. Destitute with a wife and small sons he did not know where to turn to rebuild his life. He loaded the family into his car and drove to California, settling in Long Beach.

One desperate day he went alone to sit on a rock overlooking the Pacific which, as a busy midwesterner, he had never had time to include in his life. He wondered whether life was worth the effort and had no idea what to do with the days ahead.

For a long time he sat watching the white foam rush to shore and then recede softly to await another surge forward. He contemplated the eager pressure exerted by each wave to make a landing to join the ocean. He felt rested after staring at the blue water.

This rhythm of life in action finally brought a sense of peace and he began to relate to this universal struggle for harmony that goes on with every change of season, every rainy and sunny day, even every wave that makes it to the shore. He felt his mind relaxing and the burden released as he realized he too could run hard and win, pause and let go, then move on to find a new place to begin again.

He said that day he learned the lesson as he watched the blue Pacific and began to appreciate what he still had as a young man with his health, his wife and sons. He no longer needed to accept the depression which had engulfed him for months.

As he sat on that rock he absorbed the good blue energy of sky and water and went home determined to be a winner again. As the interview ended this gentleman admitted that he was again a millionaire but now he had learned how to give back to life whereas before he only took. He had a healing that not only served himself but brought health to many crippled and sick children in the children's hospital.

This is but one example of how far reaching healing can be with color and nature's assistance.

THE ABUNDANT COLOR

GREEN

The first descriptive word you think of for green energy is abundance. What kind of energy brings growth into our lives?

All around us is the thriving profusion of living green plants and trees, bushes and flowers to which we give little heed as they constantly display their continuing growing abundance.

Green is the alliance of two great energies that combines healing blue with spiritual and intellectual yellow. This creates a combination of very high resolve and sets up for us a state of mind that would seek worthy productivity and integrity of promises made for us to keep.

One of the precious gifts of emerald energy is creativity which has no limits. It offers growth in new directions which we choose to explore. Of course we want to be interesting individuals as we expand our sights in ways not tried before. We want to do things our parents never dreamed could happen, at least not to themselves.

Meditation with green offers courage to step out to

a future ready to receive us abundantly because we know it is there. I cannot agree with the psychiatrist who said that before we are given a large opportunity we receive small chores to see if we can handle success.

Friendly and high spirited green energy invites us to share all that we find here. If you live in the concrete world of the highrise you go to the park on a day off to relax or rest or picnic. When it is time to go home you feel a sense of peaceful satisfaction although you may not be sure why this sense of harmony has come to you.

Green shakes out the tension and renews a mood of belonging in our blue and green world for balance and good feelings. The cobwebs disappear as you lie on the grass contemplating the sky with fleecy clouds gently floating overhead. Or if you walk an old trail in the mountains through the trees to view a valley far below you enjoy the waving fields of green growing things.

In California it is always thrilling to look down upon an orchard of young orange trees and sense how generous indeed the world is when we take time to appreciate its outpouring.

Notice the variety of shades of green that have to do with growing things, many of which we eat and enjoy. There is lettuce green, apple, pea, grass, olive, leaf, sea, bottle, forest, emerald, avocado and hunter green. Most of our fruits grow from their pastel blossoms to a firm virescent shade before ripening into a red apple, yellow banana, or orange.

As the happy gardener enjoys his green thumb so

does the golfer relax as he walks the rolling hills of the golf course. Wherever there is green energy we feel the freshness, freedom, peace and space for enjoyment of the abundance we find around us.

When smokey or browned shades are added to green energy it loses its crisp, fresh power and is greatly reduced, as with other color which is dark-toned. Use clear colors when you meditate for a sharp focus on your genuine desire for the best possible response.

One colorist has written of green energy as the purifier and master mechanic that renews damaged parts. It does indeed produce growth after healing has taken place through bringing the mind/body/spirit into a state of harmony and balance.

The discipline of growth is that one stands tall for his values and ethics in every department, at home and in the field. The discipline of growth means also that one is ready to accept new avenues of thinking and action to make a personal life that is self confident, guilt free and happy.

What would happen to a plant if it refused to allow the bud to form or the flower to open, which is its total reason for existing? Many times one holds back the dawn of a wonderful new experience because of fear or lack of self assurance.

With your meditation will come a feeling of the need to act alive, to allow exertion and activity to both give and receive life's blessings which are more bountiful than we suspect. Don't give up your share for lack of knowing it is there waiting.

As an aside I feel the twenty-third psalm is a better prayer than the one we think of as giving us our daily bread. Bread is not a signator of abundance but of limitation, of restriction. For meditation use "He leads me to lie down in green pastures."

Another abundance meditation also comes from the psalm in the words, "My cup runs over." We need change our thoughts and inner awareness from too little to more than enough. Bring to your well not a thimble for that small swallow leaves you thirsty soon again, but bring a generous cup which is designed to hold all your good in large measure. Your thoughts will make it so.

Now we realize that the energy waves of abundance go far beyond the idea that money is the solution to all problems. It may in fact be the creation of more problems than it solves. There are words which we often use instead of the all encompassing abundance. These include: prosperity, wealth, riches, affluence, surplus, fortune.

You may feel that of course you would like a fortune. What would enrich and fill your life better is accepting your abundance in all the areas of living, including good health, a happy family, a successful career, many friends, love and freedom with growth and happiness ahead. Bring this magnificent word into your speech, mind, heart and spirit to express your own potential and expectations that may seem magical now.

In your own words write in your green pages in your notebook several short ideas which you can think about as you move into this powerful energy. Then after the general statement you may add specific desires which may be a child who needs work or a family down the street who needs help.

MEDITATION ON ABUNDANCE

1. I accept the good intended for my life and know my cup runs over with the abundance that is universally present. I reach out to receive this gift and I in turn pass it along to others in understanding and love. I accept new growth and the discipline necessary to accomplish this for a life full, pressed down and running over and I give thanks for this understanding.

2. I know that my abundance has been prepared for me and I think and feel the knowledge I need to put this into daily life is being given to me. I enjoy my abundance in every way as I make it flow through the life with self confidence and love. I do appreciate this great gift.

EXAMPLE

A woman owned a large downtown restaurant but was unhappy because she also owned a large home that required many miles of driving often late at night. She was disturbed about what to do because she did not want to give up her home and worried about it being empty so much of the time.

After many meditations she came to realize that she

was afraid to live alone and there was another solution if she could accept it. She moved to a new downtown tower apartment near the restaurant, where she loved to spend a great deal of time working with the staff and greeting customers.

She now felt safe and relaxed about the hours of work and wondered why she had resisted the change. Meditation cleared her priorities and she found new harmony and abundance in "a time which had been choking her before," as she expressed it.

THE BLENDED COUSINS

TURQUOISE

The happiest of cousins is the blending of quiet and responsible blue with the lavish overflowing of abundant green. The result of that mating created a coloration of such genuine good humor that it has no negatives anywhere in its chart.

One sees only success with a high level of consciousness that refuses to be ignored even if used only in small areas of a room or as an accessory on the person. You always know when turquoise is present and expects to be recognized as a friend.

I have not found that this favorite blend is mentioned as having any value by others working with color, but it is everything that blue as the healer and green as abundance could hope for.

You can work with turquoise because it makes a clear, clean statement of vitality and strength. It not only heals, reunites, renews, but it does all these things with a sweet song that cannot be ignored. It makes no apologies for the fact that it is alert, happy, fresh and eager to please you.

Put it high on your list when you set up your meditation notebook.

PURPLE

The most elegant color on the chart, purple is the combination of two powerful energies individually, red and blue.

Purple was a late discovery in the world of color and when it was first used the royalty alone had exclusive use of its beauty. Peasants could only gape and admire the purple robes furred and bejeweled which were worn by the aristocracy.

Even today flowers bearing the royal color are more rare than other pinks, reds, yellows found in the florist shop. Orchids and lilacs are most precious in rich or gentle lavenders. While couturiers have popularized a range of shades labeled wine, dubonnet, mauve, grape, plum, amethyst, eggplant, the strength of a straight combination of red and blue is challenged and not meditation material.

Purple represents a heavy personality with much pomp and circumstance implied. When the saturated purple tone is reduced with innocent white, this gentler nature seems inspired, idealistic, but lavender continues to retain a mystical quality. When there is much pink in the final tint it speaks of love.

Lavender is said to be in the healer's aura and this must be because one leads with love to help others define their self worth and find a whole life filled with abundant happy living.

BEIGE TO BROWN

Many of the animals are furred or shelled in earthen tones or camouflage mottling because they need this disguise to survive from predators seeking a meal. The ermine fox, brown in summer, wears his luxury white fur during the Arctic winter.

Today it is not necessary for mankind to follow the animal pattern for the need to be indistinguishable from the ground. He has no reason for muddled mixing of colors.

This negative lack of energy is frequently found on the individual of low vitality and poor self image. An active person finds the bland no color look depressing and has a desire to change a job, school, or even a partner whom he doesn't see.

In Workshop many creative ideas came about through the examination of different colors and combinations. When we first began to use color folios to pass around the group, the negative and lost colors began to emerge.

When members chose their own color sheet with the lights turned on before the room was darkened for meditation, they felt the reaction from the color they had chosen and got response. Blue gave healing, pink filled their hearts with love to send out.

When we passed a folio of sheets in darkness and asked each one to take the top sheet, they struggled to learn what color they were holding. Soon they asked to eliminate all drab shades, grey, tan, brown, dark mixed unpleasant sheets.

When lights came on again there were comments: "I got nothing. It was a blank. I wanted to be happy and instead felt depressed with my sheet."

Seeing the non-color in their lap gave them the answer that it was not themselves but the energy which they missed and could draw no good from.

When members received a single flower for meditation they might take the blossom back to its seed, feel very small and want to be planted in the earth in a sunny spot in the garden. Feeling alone the urge came to push up the earth and welcome the sun, see how other flowers nearby were doing and what color they would become. Above the ground was much nicer than being a loner seed in the earth and being green made them want to expand and grow.

During the 1960's, a period of much uncertainty, American designers were turning to a scheme of whole projects, homes or commercial work, in a range of neutrals. Beige decorating ran rampant and after photographing expensive bland interiors for some time, curious I asked a fine designer, "When do you think color will be seen again?"

The young designer had an exquisite color sense but he now looked startled and did not know how to answer. I felt it was sad that he too was caught in the no-color look which any housewife could throw together if she were color blind. Those sterile interiors must have driven the owners to begin making changes as soon as the bills were paid.

EXAMPLE

In the early 1970s' my home was rented with the option to buy and two years later I moved back home. I found that the entire home from living room through the bedrooms had been mopped with what the tenant called "mud" color paint. Mud was a terrible choice because everything went wrong for her after such painting madness.

For some time I was not able to do anything about changing the color and still wanted to sell the property. Gradually I began to repaint one room at a time and several years later completed the job to my taste. Then I realized that I no longer wanted to leave my home which was now very nurturing.

The lesson for me was that the mud color made me wish to get rid of the house. It was totally incompatible with my feelings. We do receive color energy, or lack of it, from our surroundings.

Don't select something neutral because it goes with everything because the truth is it offers nothing in energy.

MEDITATION

Quiets the mind and relaxes the body.

Helps us stop scattering our energy.

Permits us to tune in to a deeper well of enrichment.

Stretches the whole being through expanded consciousness.

Encourages new imagery, flexibility and synthesis.

Offers new experiences in awareness through perception.

Harmonizes the symphony of mind, body and spirit.

Mirrors who we are through reflection on our world.

Presents the potential of what we can achieve.

Changes our behavior pattern to flow more easily.

Shows us that our reality is what the mind believes.

Unlocks creativity through increased perception.

Recognizes that security is an inner strength.

Heals the body through acceptance of wholeness.

Stipulates that we are one with the life force.

Expresses the depths of joy man has available.

Becomes great fun to practice daily.

And takes us to our Source.

PAINT YOUR PORTRAIT

Marika McCausland is an Egyptian woman living in London with her husband where they give lectures, demonstrations, in the practice of holistic healing.

She told me of many effective treatments she had given and I want you to know her unusual technique. A meditator can do it, as we did in Workshop, with as many sessions as one feels advisable to complete the needed results.

I do not know how long the session lasted which I had with Marika that afternoon. Although I heard her words as she instructed me to study and paint the figure she asked me to place on the canvas in my mind, I was in a different space and totally united with the painting I worked with.

Sitting in a lounge chair with Marika beside me on a small stool, I took several deep breaths and closed my eyes. Following is my version of what happened in London. Since I had no specific problem to work on we chose harmony as the theme for treatment.

"Gently she explains that the sitter has caused the problem to exist through the mind and emotions, through lack of experience or understanding. The

body knows how to heal itself and is continually doing this anyway, it is possible for the person to rid himself of any illness or distress which has become a burden.

Because of her explanation, the problem on the screen is obviously one that can now be changed inwardly, once it is confronted and understood. Marika feels that she is joined with the sitter and knows exactly how far she can work in each session. If the need is deep or terminal, she will do as much as possible each time, being careful never to overcrowd the psyche of the sitter.

Since there was no specific problem to resolve in my session, Marika told me to imagine harmony in all areas of my life.

'Now take up an imaginary paint brush and begin to paint the figure you see seated on the canvas,' she suggested.

Mentally I felt the brush in my hand. How easy this would be to change anything I desired! I began to choose colors that are my favorites to paint the figure. Under continual direction, I dip into soft shades and stroke the canvas. I see a spot that needs brightening and decide to add more emphasis over there. Ah, that helps.

Having a good time with the brush, I heard Marika's instructions, 'Now be sure to cover the figure completely with the lovely colors you have chosen. Repaint as you want her to be, and do it with love.'

The brush moves to make a sharper separation between the figure and the white background, which seems a bit fuzzy in one spot. Now the outline becomes much clearer to me. Unaware that these thoughts are *not customary conscious decisions, I know only that I am having a joyful time working with my portrait.*

I hear her words, 'Now bring every part of your painting together and you will find a loving and completely harmonious person. Having renewed this person, please envelope her with light. This is a clear spiritual light which enfolds the entire figure. It brings you energy and love, the opportunity for you to be what you have painted on your screen.

You will now reunite the person you recognize as yourself on the screen with the person in the chair. Please take a few deep breaths.' "

If you can honestly work with your brush to blend the colors needed for change or improvement into your canvas it will indeed bring you what you seek. Remember no one changes your portrait but yourself. Paint one proud to show the world but better yet, paint one proud to enjoy for your whole life.

GAMES TO PLAY

Color was always presented as energy and fun. As members learned color decoding they interpreted the technique for their own self help and expanding awareness of their world.

Many games were created to encourage this awareness. If one expressed a dislike for some color and had no reason which made sense, we worked through the positive and negative ideas presented. Ultimately they came to see and value every tone and shade and our color march proceeded.

Our choices for colors told us more than we had ever realized about the inner self which we tried so hard to keep hidden. Now the feelings of release and flexibility made the games a source of delight. Try it for yourself and you will know what we mean.

Members moved away from negative shades to both brighten their own appearance and change the mental outlook. On one occasion they listened to a huge pink conch shell and talked about how happy it had been in the sea and how much all the inhabitants of the sea loved the freedom of their environment.

Another evening they held small round Japanese

rice bowls and in the darkness began to describe the sense of healing which they received as they caressed the bowls, only to discover they were designed with blue patterns when the lights came on.

One can meditate with colored candles, choosing pink for love of life, green for abundance for oneself and others, blue for healing. Letting the color become imbedded in consciousness strengthens your feelings and gives affirmation to the purpose of your direction.

Blowing bubbles is an easy mental game to play alone when you sit in the silence after you have completed your meditation and feel very relaxed and peaceful. As you visualize the floating bubbles glinting in the colored lights, begin to add your own special color to energize each one that you send out, whether for better health, personal relationships, more abundance.

Bubbles is a happy game to set in motion if you desire a career change or are planning a college program after years have passed.

Bodily we all exist in a field of light, seen or unseen, but that in some mysterious manner identifies us as individually as our fingerprints. We are light in motion, patterning every breath with color which identifies our thought. This light displays a billboard of character and attitude, our disposition to be happy and creative.

In your notebook design a color ladder or insert a color wheel from the paint store. Write in each words that represent the five senses. What does yellow taste like, how does blue sound, what does red feel like and so forth.

On another chart you can rate each color according to your personal awareness of its energy level. For each this will be a little different but the project may surprise you because it affects your daily life in many ways you are not now aware of.

It may take a little time to discover all your color quirks because they often represent ideas long suppressed, ignored, or tied to an old superstition.

An example about a repressed idea which the woman was not aware of happened one evening during meditation when the telephone rang. She said she could not meditate and became nervous at the ringing. We discussed why my telephone made her nervous.

Finally it came out that she feared the telephone and it always frightened her when it rang because it brought bad news. After group discussion about what good news she might hear, she admitted that she would love to hear from her family who had been away some months. We helped her realize the messsenger she feared could bring good news if she was willing to accep it. One member suggested she get a "good news" color for her phone and we ended by laughing about her quick conversion.

EXAMPLE

On occasion a table was filled with words cut from magazines and members were asked to take several that most represented themselves. They selected a colored sheet to paste their words on. As instant artists they organized designs, built words climbing a ladder, formed pyramids with goal words at top, formed circles to show the eternity of their pattern.

Most of them were well in touch with the question we always kept in the foreground: Who Am I? when they described what the sheet they held up meant.

Once when we played this game an out of town guest was included in the evening meditation. Words on the table included love, great, bizarre, sorry, happy, power, hostile, eager, strong, friendly, disappointed, useless, and so on.

The newcomer chose a scarlet sheet and filled it randomly with heavy self-accusative words. Group members were startled but remained tactful when he raised his sheet to explain glumly, "This is how I feel." He went on to admit he had no intention of changing his outlook on life which was desperate and disagreeable.

GEMSTONES

Certain gemstones and metals have been claimed as magical for healing or bringing back a lost love. While color energy is indeed alive it is best to know that all jewelry is for showing its radiance and because human beings like to decorate themselves.

No single gemstone or metal bracelet has power to heal a disease or dispose of an enemy you want out of your life. If the mind hurts and abuses the body then the mind must also be the healer to restore. Color energy will keep you aware of the direction you wish to follow.

If you don't have diamonds to wear you can stand in the rain and love every pear shaped drop of the special gem from above. Know how many jewels you share with nature without ever being burdened to buy insurance or stow them in a vault. The emerald of the sea or a sapphire or turquoise sky are yours to gloat over all the days of your life.

Gemstones are a symbolic way to express emotion to represent our birthday or come from a place we have visited. Alexandrites from Russia or pearls from the Orient absorb your own vibrations when worn.

EXAMPLE

There is only a negative example to give you with gemstones. Once at a white elephant sale by my club I selected a strand of beads because they looked pretty and I had nothing that color in my costume jewelry. However I was never able to wear them and felt uncomfortable when I tried about twice.

One evening we did a psychometry game after our work with meditation and a woman had this string of beads. Her reaction was like my own. She felt the beads had sadness and were very negative and after her response I threw the beads away.

A student experiment in the Soviet Union asked that colors be rated for sensation. Although no scale was given the response interests us because it shows the difference in cultures and the traditions that we are often not aware of.

The students rated red as a color that burns and is too strong. They liked orange for its warmth but thought yellow had little to offer and only slightly warm.

A cool color was violet and they described it as pinching. In our reaction to violet and the purple family we recognize a royal background but perhaps that is what pinches in a classless society.

It seemed odd that they described green as a neutral when we see it as a growing abundant color which brings much inspiration to creative activity.

No dark shades were mentioned in the report and since that is their natural garb for long cold winters it must engender some sensations. Perhaps the darkness for them means protection, we do not know. For westerners it can mean just the opposite.

Neither blue nor white were mentioned in the brief summary we read although it could have been incomplete. For us blue and white are healing and purity.

It was interesting to notice how limited the sense of color is in many lands which do not have the great variety of choices in almost everything from autos to hair curlers to clothes. In the World Book Encyclopedia (p. 664) there is a statement that experts estimate there are ten million distinguishable shades.

COLOR INTERPRETATION

RED   — high energy, passion, violence, anger, obsession, courage determined, danger

PINK   — loving, nurturing, compassionate, consiliatory, tender, faithful, trusting

ORANGE   — warm energy, motivating, good faith

CORAL   — quiet energy, reassuring, open, stimulating

YELLOW   — peace, intelligence, wisdom, spiritual knowing, celebration,, faith

GOLD   — treasured, illuminated, glowing, sunshine

BLUE   — healing, wholeness, renewal, balance

GREEN   — abundance, growth, vitality victory, aspirations,

TURQUOISE — alertness, well-being, perception, healing prosperity

PURPLE — proud, aloof, enduring, respected, distinguished

LAVENDER — warm caring, individuality, nurturing of self

BROWN — earthy, fearful, depressed, selfish, dirty

GREY — bland, languishing, clouded, weak, adrift

BLACK — unknown, mysterious, repressed, afflicted, death

WHITE — purity, chastity, integrity, clean, idealistic

Blended indefinite shades reflect two colors which are confused in indicating a true response. Coarse, smeared or darkened shades indicate a challenge to health problems that need healing; anger, greed or selfishness that need to be forgiven and forgotten to cleanse the aura.

Write in your color notebook an example of how each of the above descriptive words will work for you in color meditation.

Decide what your color imprint will be and what it will say to you, about you and for you.

GROUP MEDITATION

One of my first experiences with meditation came years ago when a friend took me to a private home where we found some twenty adults sitting on cushions in a darkened living room. Only candles burned on a small table in front with one chair beside it.

After a few minutes of silence a young man came to sit on the chair and play softly on what appeared to be an ancient lyre. After he strummed for a few minutes, there was a long period of silence. At the end of the hour everyone seemed to rise in unison and quietly we left that peacefilled room.

As we drove home I asked, "Why did they just go there to sit in silence for an hour?"

My friend replied, "That hour may be the only time all week when they have a chance to be at peace with themselves."

It takes a few meetings for many people coming together with their high vibrations and often deep needs to meld and mellow for the single purpose of cleansing and redefining their desires. Ultimately they come to relish this silent time to seek inner wisdom which becomes a powerful force for life's smooth transitions.

Group meetings set up a rhythmical pattern that keeps you in tune and on course with images you seek to accomplish.

Groups come in all sizes over two. They take any format that numbers find most comfortable, well directed and productive. Six to a dozen people is ideal because it gives everyone time to speak and many questions are raised and discussed among the group.

In our Workshop the members were told each one made his own decisions as to how he would direct his life. Meditation was intended to be personal, goal setting, and deeply satisfying to fit one's values, desires and natural characteristics.

Our group turned in a fine example of the way intelligent adults develop a keen awareness of themselves and their world through sharing each individual's meditation. Normally meditation in the Eastern style is not openly discussed. Our joy in expressing immediately after meditation what was seen, felt, tasted, whatever, fit beautifully our plan of action.

Each evening introduced a new theme. As we met there was anticipation as one always said, "What's doing tonight?" How they responded and what they learned about themselves was sometimes expected but often a big surprise. It might bring laughter or tears, elation or concern that one did not learn the lesson sooner. Some spectacular results came about as these gems of thought surfaced and were put into action over the years.

In fact as the leader I questioned whether such growth was because this was an educated, creative and intelligent group of people who just happened to come together. That was not entirely the case.

After closing the five-year Workshop with many members participating the whole time, I felt it necessary to replicate the technique at a University of California Los Angeles evening class with a mix of students and adults who had never met the leader. Again, several surprises and special happenings occurred between September and June which vindicated and verified the process we used for meditation.

In *Meditation,* Bradford Smith writes, "The world would be transformed if everyone paid as much attention to his real as to his bodily self."

He discusses group meditation and calls it "uniquely strengthening and suggests one find a non-religious group. I agree with his idea because that was the experience of our Workshop when a dozen people showed up with all the religions you can name and one who insisted he was an agnostic.

To practice meditation without any creed or dogma dragging you through restrictions and limitations according to who said what a few thousand years ago, you do find it strengthens your personal faith, whatever that may be. For this reason few religious references are given in this book.

Your own spirit blossoms and with meditation you develop a strong and curious faith about everything of moral value. You may want to sample several faiths to determine which one is for you and then you become a member of that church, to be a most devoted ally of their teaching.

Many kinds of meditation groups are forming as we near the next century but the group that works out its own agenda can determine the needs of those present rather than follow a set formula made by another. This invites everyone to contribute and thus leads to higher consciousness and self discovery.

The meditators found they loved sharing what was received and evaluating it with what others chose to explore during the same period. One said, "It really shows how individual everyone is when we start with the same idea and get such wildly different answers."

They were asked to take the idea of their meditation home and work on it for the rest of the week and report back if there was new understanding. What they learned best was to listen, listen, listen to their inner knowing selves.

They began to understand that spirit was a personal guide and protector, the real source of the answers they needed at any time. They learned to never pressure another to join or make decisions they were not able to accept. A few who found it painful to face past mistakes or did not want to change their present rocky pathway for a smoother lifestyle dropped out. The level of each individual consciousness has to make the choice about whether change is worth the effort and the goal is worthy of the struggle.

If someone asks, "Why does everything work so well for you?" you are aware that your silent time has become dramatically effective. Your good is showing up on the outside.

You do not have to be in a group to do Color Meditation if there are not those around to join once a week. You can sit silently and make it a special event once or twice a day for very effective inner growth. You learn quickly to surround yourself with a sense of unity as you tune in to bring mind/body/spirit to at-one-ment with universal harmony.

Know that you are striving for something good that is specific (not just anything will do); second, you have faith in yourself and the technique you use; third, you work with it until it becomes a natural pattern that is simple and a joy to follow.

In so doing you answer the three basic questions: Who am I? Where am I going? How do I get there?

Keeping the questions in the right sequence is important because there can be entanglements when one wants to jump at number three without first knowing who he is or the right path to take. One of the great riddles of the universe is "Why?" Keep asking the question and watch your awareness expand for your personal growth.

Those who already have the gift of knowledge about the sensitivity of light and color could well lead a group into meditation. There is some scattered material at the libraries and bookstores, but not nearly enough. Scientists are much further ahead in the study of sound waves than in color waves.

Meditation alone or with a group is a personal journey which makes the revealing of who and what you are a long term activity and not accomplished in a few lessons. Give yourself time to find out all you can about this special you.

EXAMPLE

Early in 1970 while on the Stanford campus to do an interview, I was asked if I had ever seen the chapel. On leaving I stopped there and went inside to sit near the front.

As I sat quietly a blue mist submerged me in peace. My thoughts were undirected as I listened to what might be received.

Soon there was heard a faint sound that never grew louder but became more distinct as a gentle rush of whispers. The concentrated intensity of this baffled me and I asked inwardly: What am I hearing?

The time frame was the 1940's which seemed odd but I did not question for the muffled mingling of thousands of ardent prayers was now evident. These deeply emotional unspoken prayers came from parents, students, professors, over weeks, months, years as they sent love and safe passage to dear ones.

This compellingly irreversible yearning was a prayer that care and protection be transferred from the faithful hearts of the senders to far-away sweethearts, husbands, sons and daughters, friends, all those who served in distant fields.

After three decades this immense energy still overflowed the chapel with overwhelming love. The violence of the 1970's was not present that day either because that hostility was stil unresolved, or more likely because I had opened a different page in time to hear unspoken words whispered like leaves in a forest blown by a fire storm. Finally all became still as I rose silently and left the Stanford chapel.

AURAS

Just as we have never actually seen ourselves face to face, so too we have never seen our aura. It is that subtle emanation both from the head and the body which is called the living map of the individual.

For centuries there have been a few highly sensitive ones who could see this seemingly invisible and highly descriptive coloration which moves with constant pulsating color to define our thoughts and character, our health and state of life.

From the Latin, aura indicates the air and from the Hindu it means the spokes of the wheel flaring from the body which is the hub. S.G.J. Ousley in *The Power of the Reyes* writes, "By the study and examination of the aura of a person it can be determined easily what color vibrations the subject is most deficient in and what colors should be worn constantly on the body in some form."

Knowing your color vibrations and seeing or having a color near may remind you of its meaning but the act of wearing it constantly may not change your mind or desires and may bring no improvement into your life. A bright color cannot polish up your aura if you are addicted to negativity, disease, poverty, tobacco, alcohol or drugs.

The power of color is that you use it in an affirmative manner. If any of the above evils hold you in bondage and you do not choose to change, nothing will happen in the aura. Improvement is an inside job and not a new wardrobe.

Today's world considers stress almost a necessity because we have deliberately processed chaos into consciousness. We often refuse to resist the cacophony of bombarding negativity and sometimes even invite it through crashing sound and compulsive artificial pressure.

If we do this with sound, are we also turning on and off the color waves which can bring us the most happiness and peace because we do not understand what color means?

Keep an active and healthy aura around you through the thoughts you express and the things invited into your life. It is said a child has a white aura that develops gradually as the quality of the personality emerges. If a young child shows color in the aura it is a carry-over from a former life and suggests the direction he will take as he grows and is led into adulthood.

Aura readers believe each one of us has a characteristic color that is fundamental to our life. This basic ray never changes and is established firmly in the personality. A blue mist pulsing around the body indicates a healthy person. A muddied aura, dark or blanked out in spaces, shows disease of mind or body or a low character. Weak auras reflect poor energy and a being with little purpose or desire to live.

As we introduce color clues into consciousness it is

possible to charge our energy and create a new glow of contentment that moves us to greater appreciation for the talents and potential we have already.

There are several versions of how far the aura extends from the body. Some think a few inches while one writer states it is two feet. Others believe a foot is enough. Perhaps the strength of one's aura has something to do with its length and in that case the active creative human being will show more energy flowing.

Scientists tell us that we do not believe a thing until they have proven it true by replication in the laboratory. In this event they will one day learn to see auras and accept their value and their real importance to knowing the essence of the individual. Our doctors will keep aura records in "living color" and diagnose quickly and accurately far more than they do today both what is wrong and what cure is effective.

Auras are just as moody and moving as our thoughts with a kaleidoscope of changing tints and hues, some inviting and others dismayed. They follow the mind roving the individual's world both consciously and subconsciously.

Some believe that an aura may even beckon one across the room without a reason in the world being evident. Some day science may tell us why two people can fall instantly in love and both are quite aware of what has happened. It is a wonderfilled sensation of meeting vibrations you have known before.

In *The Symphony of Life* by Donald Hatch Andrews, he states the surface of the body radiates energy in hundreds of different hues in a quinary sub-sub-base range of invisible light. Since the body is constantly bombarded with sound, heat, light waves, it does not seem inconsistent that we really do wear a flag of identification wherever we go.

Those who work as practitioners or healers in a spiritual or medical situation often hear stories about a parent or friend who drains their energy and saps their good intentions to be of help. Every time one is around this weak individual there is a sense of being submerged by the other's needs.

If someone does this to you, get out of the way because there is nothing you can do but get them professional care. The drainer is usually not aware of the energy he/she borrows and uses from others.

A friend once complained bitterly because one she called the vampire drained all her energy, or blood as a vampire does. Other family members were unaware of the problem because vampire chose the busiest and most active person to cling to and demanded several meetings a week.

Perhaps the day science reads our auras this problem of people who cling to others for energy can be resolved. The aura as a diagnostic tool has marvelous potential for the stressed, the lonely, the unhappy, the over active, the diseased .

A soft blue haze around the body is described as indicating a healthy being with mind/body/spirit in harmony. In the auric rays there will be stronger blue and green to indicate creative pursuits and a happy frame of mind.

Black or very dark spots or breaks in the aura mean fear, distrust and "black days" while mottled reds and browns are a sign of serious illness. This means time is needed for introspection, changes in lifestyle and reevaluation.

Earlier we wrote of the healing qualities of azure skys and sparkling sapphire oceans that enfold and nurture our earth. The healer works with this and lets the patient know he can bring harmony with this gentle meditation.

What one person finds uplifting and inspired may nauseate another or cause goosebumps to a third. Response is a constant blending of auras when one rides the bus, eats in a cafe, comes in area contact with others. When we see a smutty haze obscuring the view we call it smog. Translate this smog to the pollution gathered from different areas, different sources, different people and you will begin to feel the sensations which a blending of auras of similar characters or places can cause.

For your own self-good begin to check the "vibrations" you feel as you move through the day and you will realize that you do respond to others without exactly knowing why it happens.

The definite color hues reveal for those tuned to see them our habits, talents, character, energy in the planes of our mind/body/spirit, much as our fingerprints identify us. Arthur E. Powell in his book, *The Astral Body,* writes "Colors are as intelligible as words are to men."

"If one is terrorized by a sudden shock," he writes, "the whole body is engulfed in a curious grey mist." He speaks of the brownish-green aura of jealousy or bright scarlet flashes of anger. Others describe hostility as a mucky dark red with damaged rays appearing.

Green rays are called the builder of tissue and muscle and in clear bright shades are said to be problem solvers, which is another way of saying one can develop abundance for any need. This may be why a turn around the golf course or a walk through the woods is healing because it brings answers of what to do about whatever is lacking. The lack is replaced with an abundance of choices after a restful clearing of the mind.

On a quiet walk one may almost reach a meditative state that allows the subconscious to get through the dense body.

By this time you already know that red is the most powerful energy of the spectrum we can see. Aflame with fire, heat, passion, it stimulates and excites for both good and evil. When one is in a rage everything turns red. For the individual with little self control the fire is set and may burn seering and permanent damage that can never be reversed. Muddy darkened reds indicate disease and may show low character.

The red in your aura will best be a rose -pink where love is evident with nurturing and devotion for family and friends and genuine appreciation for being alive.

Purple still reads as one of higher authority and may belong to a religious or inspirational human being. Yellow rays speak of wisdom and the spirit as we see our religious leaders crowned with golden halos.

Now we know that the aura surrounds not only the fingers and the head, but the entire body. According to a report in the Los Angeles Times, the University of California at Los Angeles in 1986 installed a machine which diagnoses illness by reading the body aura. According to the brief report it is said to be more reliable and detailed than standard EKG tests and with none of the side effects of x-ray. As the light flows from the body it is decoded for both mental and physical analysis by computer.

If you find this subject interesting, there are many old books on the theories and techniques for reading auras at your library or metaphysical book store. There is Edgar Cayce's early version of auric light. Kits offer goggles to help you see the aura. A. E. Powell's *The Astral Body* has an interesting approach to the subject.

When sufficient research is done medicine will accept aura reading as the personal way to learn what makes us tick.

Spirit needs to be rediscovered by those who substitute pills and drugs for a body and mind out of proper function. It may appear that we have traveled from the story of color energy but this follow-up needs repeating if you still question the need to love yourself, care for the entire being, evaluate what will bring you the most successful life you can have.

Color is still an elusive one, often seen but only subconsciously noted. It has the ability to appear abstract, aloof, be drab and neutral with no message. Don't believe that for a minute for color energy can lift the spirit, describe a bright personality, and tells many stories concerning genuine vibrations felt but not understood.

It resonates emotions and signals depressions, transmits every one of the five senses. It tells others what we are about whether we ourselves are aware of this give-away.

If you work in a field that uses color daily then you

are already more sensitive to its power and persuasion for alertness to color waves a flag that should not ignored. The fields of advertising, fashion, food, movies, photography, interior design, artists, landscapers, house painters are all making statements we need to recognize and translate.

Learning the message of color is like learning a new word which seems to appear everywhere once it is in mind. High affirmative awareness ticks off something in mind that responds, "Ahaaa . . . I know what you mean."

EXAMPLE

You can prove the electro magnetic energy you have in your fingers and the body also by a simple exercise. We know about the electric charge we get when we walk across the carpet but I want you to see and feel it in the fingers.

Place your hands close together but not touching. Move your fingers away from each other about six inches then slowly play them in and out as though you had a miniature accordion.

You begin to feel a tingling in the tips of the fingers as they do a little dance moving forward and backing away from each other. If you do this after meditation when you feel relaxed you will find that the sensitivity in your fingers is extraordinary.

For some months I complained that my darkroom was not light tight because when I loaded many holders I could see white light dancing about in front of me. Only months later I learned that I created that light by producing an electrical charge in total darkness.

DREAMS OF PROMISE

"I never understand what dreams mean," you shrug and try to ignore this deeper part of your being that surfaces while you sleep.

Only through sleep can the intake of the day be processed. We do not really understand what mental gymnastics and spirit conferring takes place as this input is unraveled and filed to determine the direction we must go.

Whether you are ready to accept what your dreams have to tell you is a personal decision. While you relax in sleep, you have to listen but you may not remember what transpires in your deepest emotions of what is offered to assist or protect you if you are ready to listen. We are told that we dream four times at ninety minute intervals each night.

This fertile garden of dreams nurtures, develops, promises our tomorrows. Sleep sorts out to satisfy or rectify or remind us what we are about in life. Should we not care to examine or follow our dreams, then it is like going to school with no teacher or books present. We learn nothing.

The consciousness pauses during sleep to indulge the deepest part of our psyche. Psychiatrists use dreams to learn what one's life is up to and in which direction it may be headed. Ignoring your dreams certainly wastes a mint of wonderful treasure put there for your personal use and encougement.

Suppose you have no harvest because you have never tried to interpret or recall your dreams because you say they are not reality. But most of the exemplary words we know are also intangible like courage, trust, faith, love. Dreams remembered offer very tangible potential for our guidance and abundance.

When you begin to listen and realize what your dreams are offering, you know that you have the technique to make life more wonderful.

You will recall more of your dreams when you begin to jot down even a few words on a note pad by the bed in the first moments of wakening. Dreams are often recalled only for seconds after you awaken. Put down half a dozen words to describe emotions, color, ideas in the dream.

When you get up write the more important implications as you understand them in your dream notebook and be sure to include the date. Note also if this dream is a repeat of an earlier one and why you keep it going on because you do not understand the message. When you go to sleep ask for an answer.

"What does that dream mean to me and want me to know?"

These spacy night time meanderings have their own reality which is the inner you and only you can decode it fully. You will build your own set of symbols for most dreams are obtuse, filled with symbology and come together like a jigsaw when you acknowledge their importance and seek the interpretation.

Some dream analysts have said that it takes three days to get an answer if you ask for a dream explanation of a situation. Some speedsters find it waiting for them in the morning if they are in touch with their dreams through careful study and then follow through with what is given them.

This preliminary is not to examine dream psychology but rather to identify how color fits into the dream sequence.

In *Dreams – Your Magic Mirror,* author Elsie Sechrist lists Edgar Cayce's interpretation of color in dreams. Bright and beautiful shades have happy and spiritual significance. Negative and frightening dreams are set in muddied or black colorless pits with bad implications.

Other basic color meanings are: red as the life force and sex, reduced to ros y-pink for caring, nurturing, with pink as enduring love. Blue and green are healing colors for health and fresh abundance and suggest a positive dream 'if for example, one is sitting by the seashore watching the waves tumble in to shore.

The Talmud calls a dream that is not understood the equivalent to an unopened letter. In dreams you freely write and also read what your life story has to say.

In the introduction to Dr. Carl G. Jung's *Man and His Symbols* we find that Dr. Jung resisted writing this book for some time. It was only after he had a dream asking him to reconsider that he finally gave in and accepted the task. He asked his clients to learn to interpret their own dreams for a connection with the subconscious.

Dr. Jung believes that psychologists can discover personality through word association tests but that dreams solve the neuroses in the whole psyche. Since most dreams are allegorical or fantasized they need deeper interpretation.

While there are many discussions and listing of dreams in his interesting volume, the index does not include the word color. Obviously color was not considered of great importance in 1964. Over twenty years later that has changed and color is recognized as a great assistant in interpretation of dreams.

Scientists call time the fourth dimension. We dream of people we have not yet met or of family and friends who have long left this earth. In dreaming they appear very much alive. No one knows for certain whether there are many time frames all moving about in the same space at different frequencies but invisible to each other, which is called the horizontal time frame. Or is history correct in recording one decade after the other for billions of years as the true sequence?

Our daytime reality says this latter is true. But dreams do not accept that limitation. We move in many differnt frames. Because I can have a discussion with my father who passed away in 1948 is not to say that the dream is imaginary but that it is part of the unreality of time. Freud decided that there is no time frame in the subconscious. (Psychologists use the term unconscious but since it is always on the job I prefer subconscious.)

Think of the colors you dream in as immportant to the interpretation and emotional response you have.

Color gives clues that you may want to drop into a meditation and ask for a meaning or that you can think about before you sleep, then may find occurring in your dream.

Notice the colors worn by the people you meet in your dreams and examine the mood of the setting and background. Ask questions and try to solve any confusion you have in the dream.

Because we are so individual in background, education, experience, what a dream means to one may be very different to another. For this reason the dream books listing symbology are of little use and you need to work out your own meaning for your special dreams.

Scientists and executives I have known use dreams for problem solving. "Sleeping on the problem" is exactly that. When I questioned a creative friend why he came up with such brilliant design ideas he casually replied, "I just dream them up . . . reach out and pull the one I need into the drawing board."

One desperate night I climbed into bed and wrote a brief question mentally just above my body and asked for an answer in the morning. When I awoke there was a headline answer there for my question and I was delighted. I knew it was correct.

This technique became a regular routine for me and I never questioned the correctness of the answers given. I believe learning to trust one's inner knowing is vital to making all our decisions for our best interest work perfectly. Dreams are great message senders.

Your dreams in color can be enormous help to you when you trust them completely.'

FINALE

As you reach this final page you are aware that we have examined two themes and brought them together.

First, the awareness and vitality of color energy for your meditations which will clarify your goals, expand your interests, create new excitement every day of your life.

Second, that the trinity of mind/body/spirit must be well balanced if you learn the secret of contented happiness. Each part of the trinity performs special functions which constitute and contribute to consummate harmony.

Learning and using these principles is a survival skill you will enjoy immensely for the individualized personality is self-managed and largely self-taught.

A lifetime is the process of learning to know and practice one's considerable talents while developing the unopened being with a radiant mind, sent here to test and prove itself good.

Don't paint your life by the numbers for talent comes as an inside job and never from following others. One can have the best teachers available and still sing off key. What you are is all within and how you refine and define that is what you become for the rest of your life.

Wherever you are today in thought, reach out, observe and accept all life's gifts in the reality of these two themes. There is great joy in a larger awareness that you are one with the universe and its laws, made of the same chemicals as the stars, mountains, trees, kittens, butterflies. Magically we are all bound together.

Welcome to the world of wonderful.